EDGE
BOOKS™

BUSTING BOREDOM
WITH TECHNOLOGY

BY TYLER OMOTH

CAPSTONE PRESS
a capstone imprint

Edge Books are published by Capstone Press,
1710 Roe Crest Drive, North Mankato, Minnesota 56003
www.mycapstone.com

Library of Congress Cataloging-in-Publication Data
Names: Omoth, Tyler, author.
Title: Busting boredom with technology / by Tyler Omoth.
Description: North Mankato, Minnesota : Capstone Press, [2017] | Series: Edge
  books. Boredom busters | Includes bibliographical references and index.
Identifiers: LCCN 2016031187 | ISBN 9781515747055 (library binding) | ISBN
  9781515747178 (eBook PDF)
Subjects: LCSH: Computers and children—Juvenile literature. | Creative activities
  and seat work—Juvenile literature. | Photography—Digital techniques—Juvenile
  literature. | Digital cinematography—Juvenile literature.
Classification: LCC HQ784.I58 O46 2017 | DDC 004.083—dc23
LC record available at https://lccn.loc.gov/2016031187

Acknowledgements
Alesha Sullivan, editor; Kyle Grenz, designer; Morgan Walters, media researcher;
Katy LaVigne, production specialist; Marcy Morin and Sarah Schuette, project
producers

Photo Credits
Capstone Studio: Karon Dubke, 5, 7, 9, 11, 13, 15, 16, 19, 21, 23, 24, 27, 29;
Shutterstock: Bruno Ismael Silva Alves, (grunge texture) design element
throughout, Nevena Radonja, (gaming controler, camera, video camera) Cover,
timurockart, (laptop, keyboard, mouse, ipod, speakers, phone, microphone) Cover

Printed and bound in the USA
010027S17

Table of Contents

AGE OF TECHNOLOGY

Are you feeling bored? Maybe you're hanging out by yourself. Perhaps you have friends coming over and you have no idea what to do when they arrive. You're in luck! You live in the age of technology. Computers are everywhere today. You might use one for homework or in the classroom. Cell phones are equipped with cameras, the Internet, music, and videos. With technology you can stay connected to the news, sports, and entertainment at the touch of your fingertips.

With that much technology around, how can anyone be bored? Now is the time to bust boredom with technology! You can use cell phones, computers, and cameras to create your own newscasts, go on a photo safari, or even create a video trailer for your favorite book. Are you ready? Follow the simple directions, and you and your friends can have a great time while exploring the world of technology.

CAUTION

Remember, safety first! Do not give out any of your personal information online, such as your address or phone number.

MOBILE OVERLOAD

There are over 7.2 billion cell phones in the world today. That means there are more cell phones in the world than people!

DIGITAL PHOTO ALBUM

MATERIALS

a digital camera or phone with photo capability

computer or laptop

USB cable

Grab a camera and start snapping photos to create your own *digital* photo album. You can pick any theme, such as animals, different types of plants or flowers, or your favorite places around town. Or just take pictures of anything you want! You'll have a digital photo album filled with great shots that you can share with friends and family.

TIP:

Before taking a person's picture, ask them first for their permission.

1 Ask an adult's permission to use a camera or a cell phone with photo capability. If you don't know how to use the camera or phone, ask for instructions.

2 Decide the theme of the digital album. Is your family going on a trip? Do you want to get action shots of your baseball team? Your photo album can be anything you want!

3 Start snapping pictures!

4 Connect your camera or phone to a computer using the USB cable.

5 Load the photos onto the computer or laptop. Create an album, a slide show, or a screensaver from your new pictures using a basic program on your computer, such as Microsoft Photos or iPhoto.

digital—involving or relating to the use of computer technology

USB cable—a cable used to connect an electronic device to a computer; stands for Universal Serial Bus cable

BE A BLOGGER

MATERIALS

computer with
Internet access

Do you love football? Are you a movie *fanatic*? Blog about it! Blogging means writing online about a topic that you like. It's a fun way to brush up on your writing skills while sharing your opinion about your favorite things.

TIP:
Create a fun name for your blog site that lets people know who you are and what you blog about, such as www.miketalkssoccer.com.

1 With a parent or teacher's help, find a safe blogging *domain* online, and sign up.

2 Brainstorm ideas for your topic. Some of the best blogs follow a theme, such as sports, music, or cooking.

3 Decide how often you want to post. Do you want to post something every day, once a week, or once a month? It's up to you. Whichever you choose, you'll want to stay consistent so your readers know when to look for new posts.

4 Start writing! A blog is sort of like a diary. You don't have to research your topic. You can just say what you think.

TIP:
You can add photos to your blog to make it even more interesting for your readers.

fanatic—someone who is wildly enthusiastic about a belief, a cause, or an interest

domain—a subgroup on the Internet with website addresses sharing a common suffix or under the control of a particular organization or individual

SHARPEN YOUR SKILLS

When you are writing blog posts, remember to keep your writing fun and readable. Good writing tells a story, keeps the reader interested, and uses proper spelling and grammar. Try to use some short sentences and some longer sentences to mix it up.

FILMMAKING 101

MATERIALS

a video camera or cell phone with video capability

pen and paper

a few friends or family members

costumes and props (optional)

computer

USB cable

Do you have a great idea for a movie? You could create an exciting action hero film or a *documentary* about something you enjoy. Spook your friends and family with a horror film. Lights! Camera! Action!

1 Ask an adult's permission to use a video camera or a cell phone with video capability. If you don't know how to use the video camera or phone, ask for instructions.

2 Write a *script*. Every movie needs a script that tells the story and describes what the actors say and do. Be as detailed as possible so your story comes to life.

3 Assign cast roles. Get friends or family together, and give everyone a character to play. Each character should dress up in their assigned costume, if they're willing! Don't forget, you'll need a *director* and cameraperson too.

4 Turn on the camera, and start shooting the film.

documentary—a movie or television program about real situations and people

script—the story for a play, movie, or television show

director—the person in charge of making a play, a movie, or a radio or television program

5 Connect the camera or phone to a computer using the USB cable. Transfer the video file onto the computer.

6 Edit the film using a basic video editor, such as Windows Movie Maker or iMovie. Ask for an adult's help to learn the basics of the editing program.

7 Gather the cast together to watch the world premiere of your movie. Popcorn is optional!

CREATE A NEWSCAST

MATERIALS

a video camera or cell phone with video capability

pen and paper

computer

USB cable

There's a thunderstorm heading your way. The local hockey team just had a major win. There's breaking news, and you can report it! Remember, news is something that's happening right now. With the help of your friends or family, you could have a whole news team—news, weather, and sports.

TIP:
You can play the part by dressing in a suit and tie or a nice dress.

1 Ask an adult's permission to use a video camera or a cell phone with video capability. If you don't know how to use the video camera or phone, ask for instructions.

2 Decide what kind of news you want to report. Is it a big, breaking story? A big sports game? Maybe you want to do a *human-interest piece*. Decide what you like and research the topic.

3 Write the news report. Remember to include important facts about the event.

4 Turn on the camera, and give the news! You can have someone hold the camera or you can set it up on a table.

human-interest piece—a feature story that discusses a person or animal in an emotional way; a human-interest story presents people and their problems, concerns, or achievements in a way that brings interest or sympathy to the viewers

WRITING A NEWS REPORT

Your audience needs to know the facts about the news and how they might be affected. Related stories or important background information can help. You can also include emotional pieces to really connect to your viewers. To write a gripping news report, it's important to include the following:

- a good introduction to grab the audience's attention
- facts, such as the who, what, when, where, why, and how of the news event
- lots of action verbs, such as *create*, *engage*, or *defy*
- simple language

5 Using the USB cable, connect your camera to the computer to upload your newscast.

6 Share the news with friends and family!

PRODUCE A BOOK TRAILER

MATERIALS

a favorite book

pen and paper

a video camera or cell phone with video capability

computer

USB cable

Film *trailers* show new movies that will be coming to theaters. Why not make a trailer for your favorite book? A book trailer is a video that tries to convince the viewer to read the book by showing what the book is about. Have a blast acting out your favorite scenes to intrigue your viewers. Remember not to give away the ending!

1 Brainstorm what you like best about your favorite book.

2 Write a script for the book trailer. Make your trailer as real as possible. Be sure to include the book title and author and your *rating* of the book. Your goal is to make people want to read the book and find out the ending for themselves.

3 Read the script in front of the camera. You can also act out your favorite scenes from the book to spice things up.

4 When you've finished shooting the video, connect the camera to the computer using the USB cable. Upload the video.

trailer—a short preview from a movie or program used to advertise it in advance

rating—a ranking of something based on quality, standard, or performance

5 Edit the film using a basic video editor, such as Windows Movie Maker or a similar program. Ask for an adult's help to learn the basics of the editing program.

6 Share your book trailer with friends and family!

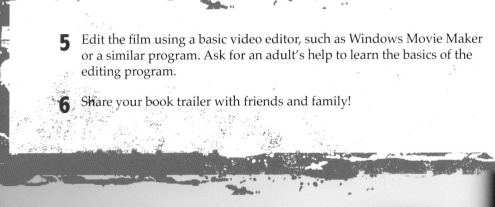

LIVE PODCAST

A podcast is similar to a blog but in an audio format. That means instead of writing out a script, you record yourself talking about whatever topic you'd like. Podcasts can add a spark of inspiration to daily life, keep you updated on political topics, and even entertain you, all at the click of a button. It's a great way for people to get information on the go. Get ready to create your very own podcast!

MATERIALS

pen and paper

voice recorder or cell phone with recording capability

USB cable

computer

1 Podcasts are usually done as a series. Think of a good topic that you'd want to talk about consistently, such as your favorite sports team or TV show. You'll want to come up with a topic that you'll enjoy podcasting about daily, weekly, or monthly.

2 Time to brainstorm about your topic! Take notes using the pen and paper. You can read from a script if you want, but a podcast should sound like you're talking directly to your listeners.

3 Hit the record button on the voice recorder or phone, and start talking about your topic. Keep your podcast short. Three to five minutes is a good start.

4 Using the USB cable, connect your recorder or phone to the computer to upload the podcast.

5 Share your podcast with friends and family. They'll be waiting for the next one!

STOP-MOTION MOVIE

MATERIALS

pen and paper

table or space to use as a stage

action figurines or props

digital camera

tripod (optional)

USB cable

computer

animation software, such as iStopMotion or I Can Animate 2

Stop-motion is a *cinematographic* technique used by filmmakers to make it look like animated figures are moving. Pictures of props or characters are taken quickly, making slight adjustments between each photo. Get ready for a fun, animated adventure using stop-motion photography!

TIP:
Find a quiet place to use for a stage. You don't want a pet or another person touching the stage until your movie is done.

1 Brainstorm a story you'd like your movie to be about. Use your imagination—your movie could be an exciting adventure using action figures or a movie that shows how to build something. Take notes using the pen and paper.

2 Create a *storyboard* for your movie.

3 Set up a stage for your movie, such as a tabletop.

cinematography—the art, process, or job of filming movies

storyboard—a series of drawings that shows the plot of a television show or movie

23

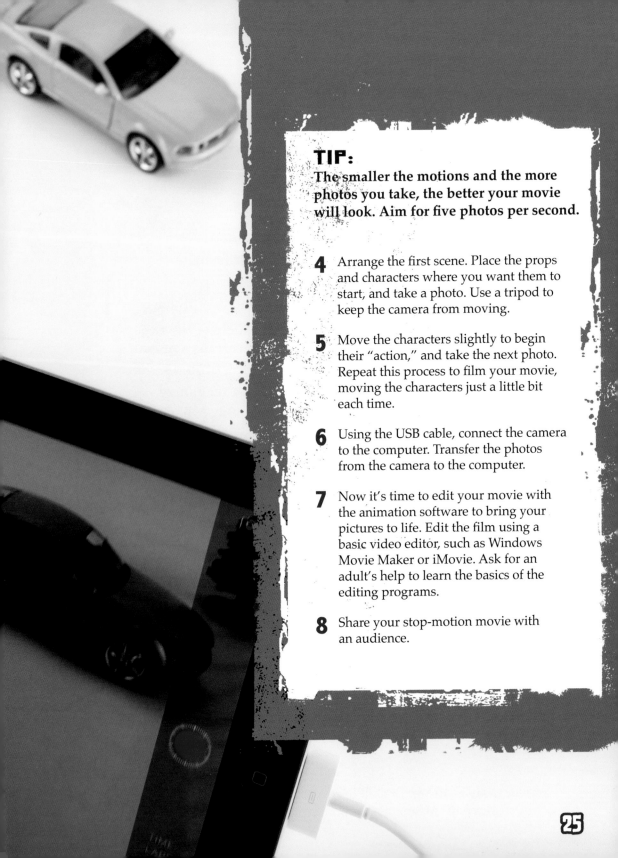

TIP:
The smaller the motions and the more photos you take, the better your movie will look. Aim for five photos per second.

4 Arrange the first scene. Place the props and characters where you want them to start, and take a photo. Use a tripod to keep the camera from moving.

5 Move the characters slightly to begin their "action," and take the next photo. Repeat this process to film your movie, moving the characters just a little bit each time.

6 Using the USB cable, connect the camera to the computer. Transfer the photos from the camera to the computer.

7 Now it's time to edit your movie with the animation software to bring your pictures to life. Edit the film using a basic video editor, such as Windows Movie Maker or iMovie. Ask for an adult's help to learn the basics of the editing programs.

8 Share your stop-motion movie with an audience.

CREATE YOUR OWN LOGO

MATERIALS

pen and paper

computer with design software, such as Photoshop or a similar program

TIP:
Too many colors can be distracting, so try and keep it simple.

Think of your favorite stores, products, or sports teams. They probably all have recognizable logos. A logo is a picture that represents a person or business. Think of some famous logos you recognize, such as the Nike Swoosh, the Golden Arches of McDonalds, or even the Batman symbol. What kind of logo would represent you? Get ready to find out!

1 What does it mean to have a good logo? Most of the logos you know and love are simple yet effective. When you see it, you know exactly what it represents. What image would represent you or your business? Brainstorm and take some notes.

2 Choose colors for the logo you want to create.

3 Start sketching. It's easier to draw out your logo first. Figure out what you like best by drawing up a few ideas.

4 Open the *graphic design* software on the computer. An adult can help you learn the basics.

graphic design—the art or skill of combining text and pictures in advertisements, magazines, or books

5 Design your logo using the design program. Do you want your logo to represent technology or nature? Maybe something sporty? Keep in mind which colors you want to use. What do you think of when you see blue? Water? The sky? How about red or green? Different colors and combinations can enhance the look and feel of your logo.

6 Show your logo to friends and family.

GIVE THIS A TRY:

Print your logo on iron-transfer paper, and make a T-shirt with your very own logo on it!

MAKE SOME DIGITAL NOISE

MATERIALS

cell phone or
tablet with access
to an app store

If you love music and you
have a few minutes to spare,
you're in luck. Grab your cell
phone or tablet and make your
own songs! It's fun and easy to
do, whether you are at home,
on the bus, or hanging out
with friends.

TIP:
The apps Figure and Ninja Jamm
are simple music-making apps—and
they're free.

1 With an adult's help, download a music-making app on the
cell phone or tablet.

2 When the app is installed, open it to begin creating music.
Once you have the basics figured out, you can personalize
your music in many ways. Pick your *rhythm* with the
drums. Then add a bass line. Don't forget to add your
singing voice too.

3 Share your songs with friends and family, and dance along!

rhythm—a regular beat in music, poetry, or dance

stimulate—to encourage something to grow or develop

BRAIN WORK

Enjoying and creating music is one of the only activities that *stimulates* your entire brain. It has been proven that music can actually make you smarter and happier. It's like doing push-ups with your mind!

GLOSSARY

cinematography (SIN-uh-muh-tog-ruh-fee)—the art, process, or job of filming movies

digital (DI-juh-tuhl)—involving or relating to the use of computer technology

director (duh-REK-tuhr)—the person in charge of making a play, a movie, or a radio or television program

documentary (dahk-yuh-MEN-tuh-ree)—a movie or television program about real situations and people

domain (doh-MAYN)—a subgroup on the Internet with website addresses sharing a common suffix or under the control of a particular organization or individual

fanatic (fuh-NAT-ik)—someone who is wildly enthusiastic about a belief, a cause, or an interest

graphic design (GRAF-ik di-ZINE)—the art or skill of combining text and pictures in advertisements, magazines, or books

human-interest piece (HYOO-muhn-in-trist PEESS)—a feature story that discusses a person or animal in an emotional way; a human-interest story presents people and their problems, concerns, or achievements in a way that brings interest or sympathy to the viewers

rating (RAY-ding)—a ranking of something based on quality, standard, or performance

rhythm (RITH-uhm)—a regular beat in music, poetry, or dance

script (SKRIPT)—the story for a play, movie, or television show

stimulate (STIM-yuh-late)—to encourage something to grow or develop

storyboard (STOR-ee-bord)—a series of drawings that shows the plot of a television show or movie

trailer (TRAY-luhr)—a short preview from a movie or program used to advertise it in advance

USB cable (YEW-ess-bee KAY-buhl)—a cable used to connect an electronic device to a computer; stands for Universal Serial Bus cable

READ MORE

Barnham, Kay. *Could a Robot Make My Dinner?: And Other Questions about Technology.* Questions You Never Thought You'd Ask. Chicago: Raintree, 2014.

Kopp, Megan. *Maker Projects for Kids Who Love Electronics.* Be a Maker! New York: Crabtree Publishing Company, 2016.

Murphy, Maggie. *High-Tech DIY Projects with Electronics, Sensors, and LEDs.* Maker Kids. New York: PowerKids Press, 2015.

INTERNET SITES

FactHound offers a safe, fun way to find Internet sites related to this book. All of the sites on FactHound have been researched by our staff.

Here's all you do:

Visit *www.facthound.com*

Type in this code: 9781515747055

 Check out projects, games and lots more at
www.capstonekids.com

INDEX